Don't Play Dirty, Gertie

Be Fair

Sarah Eason

ntary

, Inc.

D0814359

http://www.cnslow.com

It might be useful for parents or teachers to read our "How to use this book" guide on pages 28–29 before looking at Gertie's dilemmas. The points for discussion on these pages are helpful to share with your child once you have read the book together.

Enslow Elementary, an imprint of Enslow Publishers, Inc.
Enslow Elementary is a registered trademark of Enslow Publishers, Inc.

Library of Congress Cataloging-in-Publication Data:

Eason, Sarah.
  Don't play dirty, gertie! : be fair / Sarah Eason.
    p. cm — (You choose)
  Includes index.
  Summary: "This title explores the story of one child who faces dilemmas about different social situations, the choices he or she makes and the consequences of those choices" —Provided by publisher.
  ISBN 978-0-7660-4307-7
  1. Choice (Psychology) in children—Juvenile literature.
2. Fairness—Juvenile literature. I. Title.
  BF723.C47E374 2014
  155.4'1383—dc23

                                    2012037705

Future editions:
Paperback ISBN: 978-1-4644-0559-4

Printed in China
122012 WKT, Shenzhen, Guangdong, China
10 9 8 7 6 5 4 3 2 1

First published in the UK in 2011 by Wayland
Copyright © Wayland 2011
Wayland
338 Euston Rd
London NW1 3BH

Produced for Wayland by Calcium
Design: Paul Myerscough
Editor for Wayland: Camilla Lloyd
Illustrations by Ailie Busby

Wayland is a division of Hachette Children's Books,
an Hachette UK company.
www.hachette.co.uk

Contents

Hello, Gertie!

Gertie is feeling a bit grumpy. Like lots of children, she wants everything to go her way, but that isn't always fair to others.

Follow Gertie as she finds herself in tricky situations in which she must choose to be **fair**.

you choose too!

Be a good sport, Gertie

It's Sports Day and all of Gertie's friends are on another team.

It's not **fair!** Gertie wants to be with them – she doesn't even know anyone on her team.

What should Gertie choose to do?

Should Gertie:

a trip up her **teammates** so that her friends win?

b be friendly with her team and have fun racing against everyone else?

c stand with all her friends and **ignore** her own team?

Gertie, choose **b**

Don't worry – your friends will still like you when Sports Day is finished. This is a great chance to make even more friends, so you know you will have lots of people to play with.

What would **YOU** choose to do?

That's greedy, Gertie

Gertie's mom has baked a cake covered in chocolate candies.

Chocolate candies are Gertie's ABSOLUTE favorite. She doesn't want anyone else to eat them.

What should Gertie choose to do?

Should Gertie:

a share the candies with her brother?

b lick the icing so no one else will want any cake?

c sneak into the kitchen and eat all of the candies?

Gertie, choose **a**

Just because you love chocolate candies, it doesn't mean you should have all of them. Imagine how you would feel if someone did that to you! It's much better to share and be fair.

What would YOU choose to do?

Help out, Gertie

There's a new girl at
school and she looks
lonely.

Gertie is playing with her friends and doesn't want to talk to the new girl.

What should Gertie choose to do?

Should Gertie:

a make faces at the new girl until she cries?

b ignore the new girl – she can always join in if she wants to?

16

C ask the girl to join in their game?

Gertie, choose **C**

It might sometimes feel **annoying**, but looking after someone new is a really kind thing to do. Imagine what it must feel like to join a new group. Don't be afraid to share your friends. You will end up making even more friends by being kind.

What would YOU choose to do?

Own up, Gertie

Gertie has asked her sister
to help her paint Dad's shed.

But now Gertie is **worried** that Dad won't be pleased when he finds out.

What should Gertie choose to do?

Should Gertie:

a tell Dad it was her idea to paint the shed?

b say her sister painted the shed on her own?

c) hide in the shed and hope Dad doesn't notice?

Gertie, choose **a**

Honest people own up to any **mistakes** they have made and learn to say sorry. It's really not fair to blame somebody else. You wouldn't like to be **blamed** for something you didn't do, would you?

What would **YOU** **choose** to do?

Have a go, Gertie

Gertie has a math test at school today.

Gertie doesn't like math and she is **scared** she won't do very well.

What should Gertie choose to do?

Should Gertie:

a copy the answers from the girl next to her?

b pretend she is ill so that the teacher will send her to the nurse?

C try her very best?
(Numbers aren't so
bad after all!)

Gertie, choose **C**

Sometimes, you have to be
brave and work hard and
face up to things you don't
like. Usually, they turn out
to be much better than
you thought they would.

What would
YOU
choose
to do?

Well done, Gertie!

Hey, look at Gertie! Now that she can make all the fair choices, she's feeling much **happier**.

Did you choose the right thing to do? If you did, big cheers for you!

If you chose some of the other answers, try to think about Gertie's choices to help you to play fair from now on. Then it will be big smiles all around!

And remember – don't play dirty, play fair!

How to use this book

This book can be used by a grown-up and a child together. It is based on common situations that pose a challenge to all children. Invite your child to talk about each of the choices. Ask questions such as "Why do you think Gertie should be friendly to the new girl at school?"

Discuss the wrong choices, as well as the right ones, with your child. Describe what is happening in the following pictures and talk about what the wrong and right choices might be.

• Don't be greedy. It would make you sad if someone else took all of your favorite things and didn't share.

• Try to be kind to other people – how would you feel if someone was mean to you?

- Think about how others might feel if you don't play fair.

- Hiding doesn't help. It is best to tell the truth!

Talk about and act out the situations in which it's tempting to play dirty. What can be gained by playing fair? It isn't always clear to young children, and they may have lots of questions that are difficult to answer. Try to show them that it's easy to play dirty, but people will like them much more if they choose to play fair.

Explain that everyone makes mistakes, and playing dirty without meaning to doesn't make someone a bad person. Ask your child to think about how she would like her friends to behave towards her, and encourage her to behave in a similar way herself. Show her how good it feels to be generous and play fair!

Glossary

annoying—something that makes you cross

blamed—to be told that something is your fault

copy—to look at someone else's work and write it down

friendly—talking to other people and letting them join in with your fun

grumpy—unhappy and fed up

ignore—not looking at or speaking to someone

lonely—feeling all alone

mistakes—doing something wrong or getting something wrong

teammates—other people on your team

Index

Titles in the series

Library Ed. ISBN 978-0-7660-4306-0

Like all children, Carlos sometimes does things that are wrong, and doesn't come clean. He has lots of choices to make – but which are the TRUTHFUL ones?

Library Ed. ISBN 978-0-7660-4305-3

Like all children, Charlie sometimes feels a little scare He has lots of choices to make – but which are the BRAVE ones?

Library Ed. ISBN 978-0-7660-4307-7

Like all children, Gertie sometimes plays a little dirty. We put Gertie on the spot with some tricky problems and ask her to decide what is FAIR!

Library Ed. ISBN 978-0-7660-4308-4

Like all children, Harry sometimes takes things that don't belong to him. He has lots o choices to make – but which are the HONEST ones?